LEVEL A

Comprehension PLUS

Dr. Diane Lapp
Dr. James Flood

Modern Curriculum Press

All photographs ©Pearson Learning unless otherwise noted.

Photographs:
9: Upper, m.l. Peter Weinmann. 9: m.b. Johnny Johnson/Animals Animals. 9: m.r. Ron Sanford/Stone. 9: b.r., 71 t. Rich Iwasaki/Stone. 9: b.l. „Tom McHugh/Photo Researchers, Inc. 9: t.l. John Kieffer/Peter Arnold. 9: m.t. B. Lundberg/Bios/Peter Arnold, Inc. 9: t.r. R. Berenholtz/The Stock Market. 9: m.m, 11 upper „Jeff Lepore/Photo Researchers, Inc. 10: m. Stefan Meyers/Animals Animals. 10: t. Kathy Bushue/Stone. 10: b. Joel Bennett/Peter Arnold, Inc. 11: t.r. Donald Specker/Animals Animals. 11: t.l. Gary Vestal/Stone. 18: Chris Sorensen/The Stock Market. 19: E.R. Degginger/Bruce Coleman Inc. 21: t. Barbara Stitzer/PhotoEdit. 29: t.l., b.r. The Stock Market. 29: t.r. Ray Massey/Stone. 29: b.l. Peter Beck/The Stock Market. 29: m.t. Kathi Lamm/Stone. 29: m.b. Bill Miles/The Stock Market. 30: b. Michael Newman/PhotoEdit. 30: m. Jeff Greenberg/Peter Arnold, Inc. 30: m.b. Tom McCarthy/PhotoEdit. 50: Superstock, Inc. 51-52: Rocky Jordan/Animals Animals. 62: Helga Lade/Peter Arnold, Inc. 63: Tony Freeman/PhotoEdit. 63: m.l. Bob Thomas/Stone. 63: m.r David Young-Wolff/PhotoEdit. 63: l. Penny Gentieu/Stone. 65: r. „Steinhart Aquarium/Tom McHugh/the National Audubon Society Collection/Photo Researchers, Inc. 65: l. Stephen Frink/Stone. 65, 97: PhotoDisc, Inc. 66: t. Carl R. Sams II/Peter Arnold, Inc. 66: b. „E.R. Degginger/The National Audobon Society Collection/Photo Researchers, Inc. 69: l. Thomas Kitchin/Tom Stack & Assoc. 69: r. Walter H. Hodge/Peter Arnold, Inc. 71: b. Siede Preis/PhotoDisc, Inc.

Illustrations:
5-7, 93-95: Elizabeth Allen. 13-16, 49: Meredith Johnson. 25-27: Marisol Sarrazin. 33-35: Molly Delaney. 41-44: Anne Kennedy. 57-59: Pam Tanzey. 73-75: Anni Matsick. 45, 47: Betina Ogden. 37-40, 70: Erin Mauterer. 31-32, 77-80: Jeff LeVan. 81-83: Jhon Bendall-Brunello. 85-87: Laurie Struck Long.

Cover art: photo montage: Wendy Wax. background: Doug Bowles.

Design development: MKR Design, New York: Manuela Paul, Deirdre Newman, Marta K. Ruliffson.

Design: John Maddalone

Table of Contents

Comprehending Text

Story Structure

Word Study

Document Reading

LESSON 1

Following Directions

Directions tell you what to do.
Following directions can help you do things.
You follow many directions every day.

Please pack the bag.

Get in the van, please.

You follow other kinds of directions at school.

Follow this direction.

● Draw a circle around the word that matches the picture.

ball

box

Try following another direction.

■ Draw a line under the word that matches the picture.

shell

pail

Tip Directions help you know what to do. Here are some direction words: draw a line, draw a circle, write, fill in, look, read.

Practicing Comprehension Skills

Read the sentences.
Think about what the directions tell you to do.

Fun in the Sand

Mix sand and water.

Put the wet sand in a pail.

Turn the pail over.

You just made a sand castle!

1. Draw a circle around the things
you need to make a sand castle.

2. Draw a line under the picture
that shows where to put the sand.

3. What do the directions say to do first?
Draw a box around the sentence.

Put wet sand in a pail.   Turn the pail over.

Mix sand and water.

Read the sentences.
Think about the directions.

Let's Go Fishing

First, get a fishing pole and a worm.
Put the worm on the hook.
Then drop the hook into the water.
Soon you will catch a fish!

4. You want to go fishing.
Draw a circle around the thing you need.

5. What do you put on the hook?
Draw a box around it.

  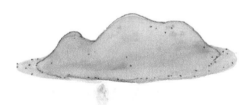

6. Where do you drop the hook?
Draw a line under it.

 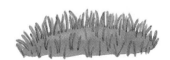 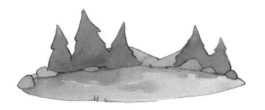

7. Write the word that belongs in the sentence.

The children use a pole to go _____.

dancing   fishing   skating

Practicing Vocabulary

Write a word from the box on each line.

sand	catch	water	worm

8. Put a _____ on your hook.

9. You can dig in the _____.

10. You can _____ a fish.

11. You can swim in the _____.

Use another piece of paper.
Draw a picture of you at the beach.
Write a sentence about your picture.

Using Details

Do you like to look at pictures? Sometimes pictures can tell a story.

This picture tells a story.

Read each question.
Circle the picture that tells the answer.

 Where is the bear?

What is the bear doing?

What does the bear use to climb?

Tip Pictures can help you when you read. When you look at a picture, think about all the things you see. Try to remember them.

Practicing Comprehension Skills

Bear Cubs

Look at each picture.
Draw a circle around the sentence that
goes with the picture.

1.    Bear cubs stay away from their mother.

Bear cubs stay near their mother.

2.    The cubs learn how to find fish.

The cubs learn how to fight.

3.    The cubs like to play.

The cubs like to read.

Write the word that belongs in the sentence.

_____

- - - - - - - - - - -

4. Bear cubs stay close to their _____ .

mother   food   friends

Read the sentences. Look at the pictures.
Think about what they tell you.

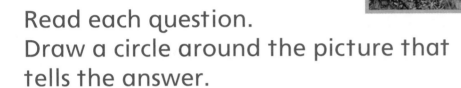

Time to Eat

Bears catch and eat fish.

Bears like fruit.

Bears like nuts.

Bears like honey, too!

Read each question.
Draw a circle around the picture that
tells the answer.

5. What do bears catch and eat?

6. What do bears like to eat?

7. What else do bears like to eat?

8. Do bears eat honey?
Draw a line under the answer.   yes   no

Write the word that belongs in the sentence.

_____

- - - - - - - - -

9. Bears eat many kinds of _____ .

trees   food   rocks

Practicing Vocabulary

Draw a line from the word to the clue it matches.

10. **nuts**   big animals that live in forests

11. **bears**   animals that live in the water

12. **cubs**   food that has a shell

13. **fish**   baby bears

 Use another piece of paper. Draw a picture of an animal you like. Write a sentence that tells about the animal.

Main Idea

What is the main idea?
The main idea is what a story is all about.
To find the main idea, think about what the whole story is about.

Draw a line under the sentence that tells what each picture is about.

● Matt has a new book.

Matt has a new pet.

■ Little Mouse lives in the country.

Little Mouse lives in the city.

▲ The dog has a ball.

The dog has a bone.

Tip **Sometimes one picture or one sentence tells the main idea. Sometimes the name of the story tells the main idea.**

Practicing Comprehension Skills

Read the story.
Look for a sentence that tells the main idea.

Jane has a new toy bird.
She likes to play with it.
Jane makes the bird go up and down.
She helps the bird fly.

Think about the story. Then read each sentence.
Does the sentence tell the main idea of the story?
Write **yes** or **no**.

1. She helps the bird fly. _____

2. Jane has a new toy bird. _____

3. Jane makes the bird go up and down. _____

4. Draw a line under the best name for
   the story.

   Jane's New Toy   Birds Can Fly   Jane Sees a Bug

Read the poem. Think about the main idea.

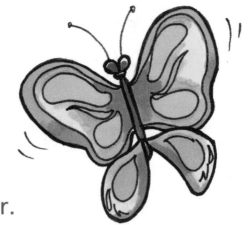

A butterfly goes by.
It flies up in the sky.
I see it fly away.
Come back another day.

Fill in the circle next to the right answer.

5. What is the poem all about?

○ The sky   ○ A flower   ○ A butterfly

6. Which sentence tells the main idea?
Write it on the lines.

It is flying in the sky.

A butterfly goes by.

It will come back again.

I see it fly away.

_____

_ _

_____

_ _

_____

7. What is the best name for the poem?
Draw a line under it.

The Butterfly   Blue Sky   Pretty Flower

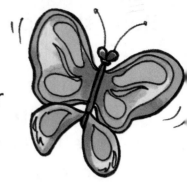

Practicing Vocabulary

Write a word from the box on each line.

sky	another	bird	fly

_____

8. I see a plane in the _____ .

_____

9. The _____ is in a tree.

_____

10. Some bugs can _____ .

_____

11. I will read _____ book.

Use another piece of paper. Draw a picture of your favorite animal doing something. Write a name for your picture that tells the main idea.

Main Idea and Details

You can learn a lot from stories. The main idea is the most important idea you learn. It tells what the sentences or pictures are all about.

Read the story and look at the picture.

This is Sara's first airplane ride.
She sits with Woolly Bear.
They look out the window.
Sara thinks flying is fun!

 Circle the name that belongs in the sentence.

Sara sits with _____.

Mom   Woolly Bear

■ Draw a line under the word that tells what the story is all about.

playing   flying   looking

Tip **Try to remember all the things a story tells. To find the main idea, think about what the picture or story is all about.**

Practicing Comprehension Skills

Read the sentences.
Think about what they tell you.

A pilot flies a plane.
Pilots go to school to learn how to fly.
They learn how to read maps.
They learn about weather.
Then pilots can fly planes to many places.

Draw a circle around the correct words.

1. To fly a plane, pilots go to _____.

   a park   school   the store

2. Draw a line under the sentence that
   tells what the sentences are all about.

   Pilots learn about air.

   Pilots have to learn many things.

   Pilots learn how to read books.

3. Draw a line under the best name
   for the sentences.

   Reading Maps   Big Planes   A Pilot's Job

Read the sentences.
Think about what the sentences tell you.

Did you ever see a blimp?
Blimps look very different than planes.
The top part is like a big balloon.
This part is filled with a gas.
The gas makes the blimp float in the air.
The bottom part is like a small box.
This is where the people sit.
Would you like to fly in a blimp?

Fill in the circle next to each correct answer.

4. What do blimps look like?

　○ big balloons　○ apples　○ small boxes

5. Where do the people sit?

　○ in the top　○ on a balloon　○ in the bottom

6. The top part of a blimp is filled with

　○ oranges.　○ gas.　○ boxes.

7. Draw a line under the sentence that tells the main idea.

Learn about blimps.　　　Blimps are balloons.

Blimps are big.

8. Circle the best name for the sentences.

Flying Things   Blimps Are Big   All About Blimps

Practicing Vocabulary

Write the word from the box that matches each clue.

balloon	blimp	pilot	plane

_____ **9.** big flying machine that floats in the air

_____ **10.** flying machine with wings

_____ **11.** something filled with air

_____ **12.** person who flies a plane

Making the
Reading
and
Writing
Connection

Use another piece of paper. Draw a picture of something that can fly. It can be a bird, a plane, a balloon, or a blimp. Then write a sentence that tells about your picture.

LESSON 5

Summarizing

When you tell about a story, you tell the important parts. You leave out the parts that are not important. You tell what the story is all about.

Read these sentences.
Think about what is important.

People wear all kinds of clothes.
When it is cold they wear hats and mittens.
When it is hot they wear shorts.
When it rains they wear boots.

People need different clothes
for different kinds of weather.

● Draw a line under the sentence that
tells the most important parts.

People wear different clothes in hot and cold weather.

People wear boots when there is snow outside.

Tip | **When you tell what something is all about, you tell only the most important parts.**

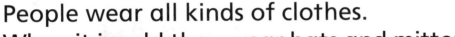

Practicing Comprehension Skills

Read the sentences.
Think about the important parts.

Lots of Hats

There are many different kinds of hats.
Some hats have flaps to keep ears warm.
Some hats are wide to give shade from the sun.
A hard hat keeps a worker's head safe
Some hats show the jobs people do.

Draw a line under the best answer.

1. Are all hats the same?   Yes   Maybe   No

2. How do hats help people?

   Hats keep ears warm.   Hats keep hands safe.

   Hats keep toes warm.

3. What is the most important thing
   about "Lots of Hats"?

   Some people do not like to wear hats.

   Some hats look funny.

   There are many different kinds of hats.

Read the sentences.
Think about what is important.

Working Shoes

Shoes can help people do their jobs.
Boots keep a firefighter's feet dry.
Sneakers help players run and jump.
Heavy boots keep a worker's feet safe.
Different workers use different kinds of shoes.

Fill in the circle next to the best answer.

4. What can shoes help people do?

○ their jobs   ○ homework   ○ wash dishes

5. What is "Working Shoes" mostly about?

○ socks   ○ different shoes   ○ sneakers

6. What is one kind of shoe "Working Shoes" tells about?

○ slippers   ○ sandals   ○ boots

7. Draw a line under the sentence that tells the most important thing about "Working Shoes."

Different kinds of shoes help workers do their jobs.

Some workers have too many pairs of shoes.

Some workers need boots.

Practicing Vocabulary

Draw a line from the word to the group it belongs with.

different

shade

shoes

warm

8. boots, slippers

9. hot, cozy

10. not the same, not alike

11. cloud, shadow

On another piece of paper, draw a picture of your favorite kind of shoes or clothes. Write a sentence that tells about your picture.

Drawing Conclusions

When you read, look for picture and word clues. Think about what you already know. Put it all together to help you understand what you read.

Look at this picture. What do you see? You know that kittens like to be petted. How do you think the kitten feels?

● Draw a line under the sentence that tells how the kitten feels.

The kitten is happy.   The kitten is not happy.

■ Look for clues in the picture.
Draw a line under the sentence that tells about the picture.

Toby will play outside today.

Toby will play inside today.

 Tip **When you read, look at the pictures and words. Think about all the clues you find. Put them together with what you already know.**

STRATEGY: Drawing Conclusions   25

Practicing Comprehension Skills

Read the story and look at the picture.
Think about the clues.

Kim's Visit

Kim and Mom are going on a visit.
On the way Kim sees some flowers.
She stops to smell them.
She decides to pick some.
Soon Kim knocks at a door.
"Hello, Grandma," says Kim.
"These are for you!"

Draw a line under the correct answer.

1. Who is Kim going to visit?

her grandmother   her mother   a friend

2. Why does Kim pick some flowers?

She wants to give them to her mother.

She wants to give them to a friend.

She wants to give them to her grandmother.

Read the story. Look at the picture.
Think about the clues.

Bill Tries to Sleep

Bill is a pig who cannot sleep.
"What is that smell?" he asks.
"Please quit singing," he says.
Bill shuts the window.
Then he falls asleep at last.

Fill in the circle next to the right answer.

3. What does Bill hear?

○ a skunk   ○ a cat   ○ a pig

4. What does Bill smell?

○ a window   ○ a cat   ○ a skunk

5. Why does Bill shut the window?
Draw a line under the sentence that tells why.

He wants to work.

It is cold in the room.

He wants to sleep.

Read the question. Draw a line under two sentences that tell the answer.

6. Why do you think Bill falls asleep?

   Bill does not hear the cat singing.

   Bill does not smell the skunk.

   Bill does not shut the window.

Practicing Vocabulary

Write the word that belongs in each group.

7. taste, hear, _____

8. rest, nap, _____

9. choose, keep, _____

10. stop, halt, _____

| sleep |
| smell |
| quit |
| pick |

On another piece of paper, write some clues that tell about a food you like. Tell how it looks, tastes, and smells. Have a friend guess your food.

Drawing Conclusions

How do you find the answer to a riddle?
First, you read each clue.
Then you put all the clues together.
You think about them again.
You find the answer.

● Read the riddles.
Draw a line under the answers.

I take care of animals.
I help them feel better when they are sick.
Who am I?

a teacher　　　　a vet　　　a clown

I like to help children.
I teach them many things.
Who am I?

a dentist　　　a builder　　　a teacher

 Tip | **Think about clues when you read. Think about things you already know. Put them together to help you understand what you read.**

Practicing Comprehension Skills

Read each riddle about someone's job.
Draw a line from the riddle to the
picture that answers it.

1. I carry a huge bag full of letters.
I bring the letters to people.
Who am I?

2. I work on an airplane.
I take people places.
Who am I?

3. I work with sick people.
I help them feel better.
Who am I?

4. I work in a shop.
I cut people's hair.
Who am I?

Read the story.
Look for clues in the words and pictures.

The Missing Ring

"Use this rake," said Mr. Lee.
"I like to help you work," said Sue.
"Take off your ring while we work," said Mr. Lee.
"I will hang it up," said Sue.
Later, Sue could not find her ring.
"Where is it?" she cried.

Fill in the circle next to the correct answer.

5. What work are Sue and Mr. Lee
    doing?

    ○ making a nest   ○ raking leaves   ○ sweeping

6. Where did Sue put her ring while she worked?

    ○ on the ground   ○ around her neck   ○ on a tree

7. Who took Sue's ring?
    Draw a line under the picture.

8. Where will Sue find her ring?
Draw a circle around the picture.

Practicing Vocabulary

Write the word from the box that matches each clue.

use	ring	huge	letters

_____

_____ **9.** things that come in the mail

_____ **10.** very big

_____ **11.** to do something with

_____ **12.** something you wear on your finger

On another sheet of paper, write a riddle.
Give two or three clues about a job someone
does. Ask a friend to answer your riddle.

Sequence of Events

In a story, things happen in order. Something happens first. Something happens next. Something happens last. When you read, think about the order of the things that happen.

These pictures tell a story in order.

● These pictures show what Dee made in art class. These pictures are not in order. Write 1, 2, or 3 next to each picture to show what happened first, next, and last.

_____  _____  _____

Tip  **Think about the order of the things that happen in a story. What happens first? What happens next? What happens last?**

STRATEGY: Sequence of Events   **33**

Read the story.
Think about what happens first, next, and last.

Dee and Robo

One night, Dee had a dream about Robo.
First, Robo went to the kitchen.
Next, Robo made breakfast for Dee.
Last, Robo washed the dishes.

1. Write words from the box to put the pictures in order.

first	next	last

_____   _____   _____

- - - - - - - - -   - - - - - - - - -   - - - - - - - - -

_____   _____   _____

Read the story. Think about the order of what happens.

A Buzzy Day

Ben has a friend named Buzzy.
First, Buzzy eats with Ben.
Then, Buzzy rides the bus with Ben.
At school, Buzzy reads with Ben.
Last, Buzzy goes to sleep with Ben.

2. Draw a line from the sentences to the numbers to show when things happen.

Buzzy goes to sleep.   3

Buzzy eats.   1

Buzzy reads.   4

Buzzy rides the bus.   2

3. What happens after Buzzy rides the bus? Draw a circle around the correct picture.

STRATEGY: Sequence of Events   35

4. What happens before Buzzy rides the bus?
Draw a line under the correct sentence.

Buzzy eats.   Buzzy goes to school.

Practicing Vocabulary

Write the word from the box that belongs in each group.

5. bedroom, den, _____

6. teacher, classroom, _____

7. draws, writes, _____

8. night, sleep, _____

dream

kitchen

reads

school

Pretend a robot visited you. On another piece of paper, draw three pictures. Show what you and the robot do. Write 1, 2, and 3 to show what happens first, next, and last.

Sequence of Events

When you read, think about the order of things. Something happens first. Then something else happens. Try to remember the order of the things that happen.

● These pictures tell a story.
The sentences tell the same story.
Write 1, 2, 3, and 4 next to each sentence to show the order.

_____ The cake is gone.

_____ Frog comes to visit.

_____ Cow gets a cake.

_____ They eat cake.

 When you read, use clue words to help you. Words such as first, then, next, and last can help you remember the order.

Practicing Comprehension Skills

Read the story.
Think about the order of the things that happen.

A Special Day

First, Jane made a cake.
Then, she went to find her dad.
"Come outside with me," Jane said.
"Now close your eyes," Jane said.
At last Jane shouted, "Happy birthday!
You can open your eyes!"

1. Show the order of things that happened
in "A Special Day." Write 1, 2, 3, or 4 on
the lines.

  _____

 _____

 _____

 _____

Read the story.
Think about the order of the things
that happen.

Sam's Surprise

by Cheryl Chapman

First, Kate made a map for Sam.
Sam read the map.
It led to a table.
Next, Sam saw two plates.
There was cake on the plates.
Then, Kate said, "Happy birthday, Sam!"
"This is good cake!" Sam said at last.

2. Read the sentences.
Write 1, 2, 3, or 4 on the lines to show
the order of things that happened.

Sam saw cake. _____   Sam read the map. _____

They ate cake. _____   Kate made Sam a map. _____

3. What did Kate do last? Fill in the circle.

○ She baked a cake.

○ She said, "Happy Birthday, Sam!"

○ She made a map.

Practicing Vocabulary

Write a word from the box on each line.

4. Kate put the _____ in the sink.

5. Sam loves to eat birthday _____ .

6. "I want the _____ piece!" cried Pig.

7. Jane _____ a big mess!

made
cake
first
plates

Making the Reading and Writing Connection

On another sheet of paper, draw three pictures about a birthday party. Write a story about the pictures. Use words like first, then, and last to show when things happen.

LESSON 10

Predicting Outcomes

Do you ever wonder what will happen next in a story? Clues in the words and pictures may tell you.

● Molly is dressed to go outside.

What will Molly do next?
Draw a circle around the picture.

■ Molly likes to make things with snow.

What will Molly do next?
Draw a line under the picture.

Tip **When you read, think about what will happen next. Look for word and picture clues. They will help you.**

STRATEGY: Predicting Outcomes　41

Practicing Comprehension Skills

Read the story. Then tell what happens next.
Look for clues in the sentences.

Ups and Downs

by Robin Pulver

Sam's sled went down, down, down the snowy hill.
"Oh, no!" Sam said.
"Now I have to pull my sled back up."
Sam wanted to go down again.

1. What will Sam do next?
Draw a circle around the picture.

Soon, Sam's feet and hands got cold.
His nose was cold, too.
It was almost time for lunch.
Jill said, "Let's ride down again."

2. What will Sam do now?
Draw a circle around the picture.

Read the story below.
Think about what will happen next.

Frosty Friends

"Help! I'm stuck inside," said Fuzzy Tail.
"There's too much snow!"
"I have a shovel to help you," said Owl.
"Thank you, Owl," Fuzzy Tail said.
"All this work makes me hungry," said Owl.
"Now I will help you," said Fuzzy Tail.
"Yum!" said Owl.

Draw a circle around your answer.

3. How will Owl help Fuzzy Tail?

4. How will Fuzzy Tail help Owl?

5. What will Fuzzy Tail and Owl do next?
Draw a line under the picture.

Practicing Vocabulary

Draw a line from the sentence to the word it is missing.

6. The boy needed ____ to get up.

again

7. It is fun to play in the ____ .

snow

help

8. A ____ goes down the hill.

sled

9. The boy went home ____ .

Making the
Reading
and
Writing
Connection

On another sheet of paper, start a story. Write your story about playing outside with a friend. Ask your friend to tell what will happen next.

Predicting Outcomes

You can tell what will happen next in a story.
Think about what you already know.
Picture clues and word clues can help you, too.

Look at the pictures.
Draw a line under the sentence that
tells what will happen next.

They ride in a boat.
They get in a car.

Dad will splash Sally.
The fish will splash Sally.

Tip | **To tell what will happen next in a story, ask, "What do I already know?" Putting all the clues together will help you.**

Practicing Comprehension Skills

Read the story.
Think about what will happen next.

 Whale Watch

Bob and Mom are on a big boat.
They want to see a whale.
"Look!" says the boat captain.
Bob and Mom see a spray of water.

Fill in the circle next to the answer.

1. What do you think the spray of water means?

    ○ A bird is flying by.   ○ It is raining.

    ○ A whale is under the water.

2. What do you think will happen next?

    ○ They will go home.   ○ They will see a whale.

    ○ They will see the moon.

3. How will Bob and Mom feel when they
see the whale?

    ○ tired   ○ happy   ○ sad

Read the story.
Look for clues to tell what will happen next.

Wet Like Whales

"The whales are so close!" said Bob.
"Wear these raincoats," the captain said.
"Why?" asked Bob's mother.
"You'll see!" laughed the captain.

Draw a line under the answer.

4. Why do you think the captain gives
   Bob and Mom raincoats?

   She wants them to stay warm.

   She wants them to stay dry.

   She wants them to eat.

5. What do you think will happen when
   the whale leaps out of the water?

   Water will splash on Bob and Mom.

   Bob and Mom will jump in the water.

   Bob and Mom will fly in the air.

6. What will Bob say when he gets home?
Draw a line under the sentence.

I saw some whales!

I saw some birds!

I saw a tiger!

Practicing Vocabulary

Write the word from the box that belongs in each group.

whale
captain
why
raincoats

7. leader, chief, _____

8. when, where, _____

9. fish, shark, _____

10. hats, boots, _____

On another sheet of paper, write an animal story. Read the first part to a friend. Let your friend tell how the story ends.

LESSON 12

Cause and Effect

When you read, think about what happens.
Think about why it happens.

Think about what happens in each picture.

The children play.   **It begins to rain.**   **They go inside.**

Sometimes when one thing happens,
it makes something else happen.
Now read these sentences.

The bug lands on Becky.
Becky waves her arm.

● Draw a circle to show what happens next.

Tip

**When you read, think about how one thing
can make another thing happen.**

STRATEGY: Recognizing Cause-and-Effect Relationships   **49**

Practicing Comprehension Skills

Read the sentences.
Think about what happens and why.

A Bee's Life

Bees get food from flowers.
A bee takes the food back to the hive.
Then the bee dances for the other bees.
The dance tells the other bees where to find food.
Bees look for food in warm weather.
In cold weather, bees stay in the hive.
Then they eat the honey stored in the hive.

Read the first part of each sentence.
Draw a line under the words that tell
what happens next.

1. Bees need food, so

   they go to a store.   they get it from flowers.   they buzz.

2. When a bee finds food,

   it dances to tell the others.   it flies away.   it hides.

3. When it is cold,

   bees sleep.   bees fly away.   bees stay in the hive.

Read the sentences.
Think about what happens and why.

A Snack for a Spider

Spiders make webs.
They use the webs to catch bugs.
A spider's web is like a sticky net.
When a bug flies into the web, it gets stuck.
Then the spider eats the bug.

Read the first part of each sentence.
Then fill in the circle next to the words
that tell what happens next.

4. The spider makes a web, so

○ it flies away.   ○ it catches bugs.   ○ it falls asleep.

5. Because the web is sticky,

○ it glows.   ○ bugs see it.   ○ bugs get stuck.

6. A spider catches a bug, and then it

○ eats it.   ○ hugs it.   ○ sings to it.

7. When a bug flies into the web,

○ it runs away.   ○ it smells pretty.

○ it gets stuck.

Draw a line under the correct sentence.

8. Why do spiders catch bugs?

Spiders play with bugs.

Spiders eat bugs.

Spiders spin bugs.

Practicing Vocabulary

Draw a line from the clue to the word.

9. A bee's house

flowers

10. Moves in the air

hive

spider

11. Pretty petals

flies

12. It spins a web

Think about something a bug does. On another piece of paper, draw a picture of it. Write sentences that tell why the bug does it.

Cause and Effect

When you read, think about what happens.
Then think about why things happened.
Look for words such as **because** and **so.**
They can be clues that help you to know
why something happened.

Read the story. Think about what happens and why.

1.

2.

3.

The boys want eggs.   **Dad cooks eggs.**   **The eggs are ready.**

Read the sentence that tells what happened.
Circle the picture that shows why it happened.

What Happened

● The eggs are
ready to eat.

Why It Happened

Tip When you read, think about how one
thing can make another thing happen.

Practicing Comprehension Skills

Read the sentences.
Think about what happens and why.

How Does a Bean Grow ?

A bean is a seed you can eat.
You can grow a bean plant.
First, you plant the bean.
Then you water it.
Make sure it gets some light.
Soon you will have a bean plant.
When beans are cooked, you can eat them.

These sentences have two parts.
Read the first part of each sentence.
Then draw a line under the words that
tell what happens next.

1. A bean is a seed, so you can

   plant it.   play catch with it.   yell at it.

2. Because you water the seed,

   a fish grows.   a plant grows.   you grow.

3. When beans are cooked,

   a plant grows.   you can eat them.   throw them away.

Read the story.
Think about what happens and why.

A Birthday Surprise

Mom and Mina whisper in the kitchen.
Dad is still asleep.
It is his birthday.
Mom and Mina are making a surprise for Dad.
Mina stirs the batter.
Then Mom cooks the pancakes.
When they bring them to Dad,
Mina yells, "Happy Birthday, Dad!"
Dad wakes up with a smile.

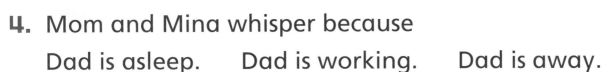

These sentences have two parts.
Read the first part of each sentence.
Then draw a line under the words that
tell why something happens.

4. Mom and Mina whisper because

   Dad is asleep.   Dad is working.   Dad is away.

5. They are making a surprise breakfast because it is

   Mom's birthday.   Dad's birthday.   Mina's birthday.

6. Mom will cook the pancakes so

   she can drop them.   Mina can stir them.

                    Dad can eat them.

Fill in the circle next to the best answer.

7. Why does Dad wake up with a smile?

○ He is happy it is raining.

○ He is happy to have a birthday surprise.

○ He does not like pancakes.

Practicing Vocabulary

Draw a line from each clue to the word.

8. get bigger, rise   **seed**

9. bean, pit   **grow**

10. hold, carry   **cook**

11. make, heat   **bring**

Draw a before and after picture. Write a sentence that tells what happened. Write another sentence that tells why it happened.

Real and Make-Believe

Some stories you read are **real.** They could really happen. **Make-believe** stories could **not** really happen. In make-believe stories, animals can talk. People can fly. Anything can happen!

● Only two of these pictures are real. Circle the picture that is not real.

▲ Look at the picture. Then read the questions. Circle the word that answers each question.

● Can raccoons really write letters? Yes   No

■ Do raccoons really wear clothes? Yes   No

▲ Is this story real or make-believe?   Real   Make-believe

Tip **When you read, think about what could be real and what is make-believe. If something in a story could not really happen, it is make-believe.**

Practicing Comprehension Skills

Read the story. Then read the sentences.
Draw a line under each sentence that is real.
Put an **X** on each sentence that is make-believe.

Jake's Pets

Jake has a dog named Bingo.
He has a kitten named Cleo.
Jake also has a goat named Munch.
Munch likes to eat grass.
Jake likes to eat cookies.
Bingo likes to eat cookies, too!
"Stay away, Bingo," says Jake.
"These cookies are not for you."

1. A dog can read.

2. A kitten can use a backpack.

3. A bird can sing.

4. A goat can eat grass.

5. A boy can read a book.

6. A boy can fly like a bird.

Read the story. Think about what is real and what is make-believe.

Space Race

by Anastasia Suen

Two rockets went into space.
They were racing to a star.
"Can we win?" Dog asked Fox.
"I see the star," Fox told Dog.
"Faster," said Dog. "Here comes Cow!"
Fox and Dog flew over the star.
"We won!" they shouted.

Read each sentence. If it is make-believe, circle the word **Make-believe.** If it is real, circle the word **Real.**

7. A rocket can go into space.	Make-believe	Real
8. A dog can talk to a fox.	Make-believe	Real
9. A fox and a dog can fly over a star.	Make-believe	Real
10. A star is in space.	Make-believe	Real
11. A cow can fly a rocket.	Make-believe	Real
12. Rockets can go very fast.	Make-believe	Real

13. Circle the word that tells what kind of story "Space Race" is.

Make-believe   Real

Practicing Vocabulary

Write a word from the box in each sentence.

star	stay	rockets	kitten

14. Special pilots fly _____ into space.

15. Sam likes to pet his _____ .

16. At night Jess watches for the first _____ .

17. When you are sick, you should _____ home.

Making the **Reading** and **Writing** Connection

On another sheet of paper, draw a picture of something that is real and something that is make-believe. Write words to tell about each picture.

Using Context Clues

Sometimes when you read, you need to
figure out what some words mean.
Look for clues in the pictures.
Other words can also help you.

● Read the first sentence.
Then circle the word that belongs in
the next sentence.

Kelly's smile looks different now.

She lost a _____.

    tooth   book

What helped you figure out the answer?
If Kelly lost a tooth, her smile would look
different.
The words **smile** and **different** are your
clues.

Tip
**When you see a word you do not know, look
for clues in the words and pictures.**

Practicing Comprehension Skills

Read these sentences.
Write the word that belongs in each sentence.
Use clues to help you.

Animal Teeth

by Wendy Pfeffer

1. Dogs and cats are _____
that have baby teeth.

animals
bugs

2. Animals lose their baby teeth, too.

   Then they grow bigger teeth just like

   _____

   _____ do.

chairs
people

3. Puppies lose their baby teeth when they are

   _____

   about 12 _____ old.

weeks
bags

4. Then new teeth _____ in.

skip
grow

Read the sentences. Write the word from
the box that belongs in each sentence.

What Makes Baby Teeth Fall Out?

by Wendy Pfeffer

| bigger | mouth | sets | teeth | room |

5. People have two _____ of teeth.

6. First, your baby _____ grow in.

7. As you grow, you need _____ teeth.

8. One by one, the baby teeth fall out of your _____.

9. This makes _____ for the new teeth to grow in.

10. Circle the word that means the same as the underlined word.

It is important to brush your teeth.

wash   drink   visit

Practicing Vocabulary

Write the word from the box on the line.

lose	teeth	mouth	bigger

_____

11. Nate's _____ is turned up in a big smile.

_____

One of his baby _____ fell out today.

_____

When you _____ a tooth, a new tooth will grow in its place. The new tooth that

_____

grows in will be _____.

Make a poster on another sheet of paper. Draw a picture that shows how to take care of teeth. Write sentences that tell what to do.

Classifying

Some things are alike in some ways.
They belong in the same group.

● Look at the pictures.
Circle the two pictures that belong together.

How do the shark and the fish go together? They
both swim in water. Does a house swim in water?

▲ Circle the two words that belong together.

sea   water   land

■ Circle the two sentences that belong together.

Bears live in the forest.

Many animals live in the sea.

You will find all kinds of fish in the sea.

Tip

**As you read, think about how things belong
together. Then you can put them in a group.**

Practicing Comprehension Skills

Life at the Pond

Many animals can be found at a pond.
Some animals are land animals.
Deer, rabbits, and foxes visit the pond
for a drink of water.
Other animals are water animals.
Fish and turtles swim. Frogs splash.

You read about two groups of animals.
One group is Land Animals. The other is
Water Animals. Write the name of each
animal in the box where it belongs.

| fish | rabbit | frog | deer | fox | turtle |

Land Animals	Water Animals
1. _____	4. _____
2. _____	5. _____
3. _____	6. _____

Read the story. Look at the picture.

Going to the Seashore

Lisa wanted to swim.
She took a tube.
Ted wanted to play in the sand.
He took a pail.
Mom wanted to sit and read.
She took a book.

At the seashore Lisa found shells.
Ted saw a boat.
Mom fell asleep.

Group some things from Lisa, Ted,
and Mom's trip to the seashore.
Write the name of each thing on the line
where it belongs.

pail   swim   tube   shells   boat   play

Things to Take	Things to Do	Things to See
1. _____	3. _____	5. _____
2. _____	4. _____	6. _____

Fill in the circle next to the right answer.

7. What list does Mom's chair belong on?

○ **Things to Take** ○ **Things to Do** ○ **Things to See**

Practicing Vocabulary

Draw a line from the sentence to the word.

8. Water animals live in a _____ .

swim

9. You can swim and fish at the _____ .

found

pond

10. The boy can _____ in deep water.

seashore

11. The girl _____ many shells.

Use another piece of paper. Draw a picture of some animals that live in the sea. Write one or two sentences that tell why the animals belong in a group.

LESSON 17

Comparing and Contrasting

Alike means how things are the same.
Different means how things are not the same.

Look at the pictures. Look at the chart.
Think about how the pictures are alike
and different.

	Alike	Different
grows on tree	✔	
color		✔

Sometimes things are alike in one way. They can also be different in another way.

Read these questions. Look at the chart again.
Circle the answer.

● Do apples and pears grow on trees?   Yes   No

■ Are apples and pears the same color?   Yes   No

Tip   **When you read, ask yourself if two things are the same or not. Then think about how they are alike and different.**

STRATEGY: Comparing and Contrasting   69

Practicing Comprehension Skills

Read the story. How are Sun and Moon alike?
How are they different?

Who Is Best?

by Susan L. Roth

Sun and Moon were talking.
"We are both round and live in the sky," said Sun.
"I am hot, and you are cold.
I am big, and you are small. I am best!"
"We both give light," said Moon.
"I help people see at night.
You help people see in the day.
We are both best at what we do."

Write **X** in the boxes to show how
Sun and Moon are alike and how they
are different.

		Alike	Different
1.	Size		
2.	Give light		
3.	Time when you see them		
4.	Shape		
5.	Live in sky		

Read the story.
Think about how trees and flowers are
alike and different.

Trees and Flowers

Trees and flowers are plants.
They grow in the ground.
Trees are big.
Flowers are small.
Trees have green leaves. So do flowers.
Trees have thick bark.
Flowers have thin stems.
Trees and flowers are living things.

Look at the box. Write the words that only
tell about trees on the lines under **Trees.**
Write the words that only tell about
flowers on the lines under **Flowers.**
Write the words that tell about trees **and**
flowers on the lines under **Both.**

| plant | leaves | big | small | bark | stems |

Trees	Both	Flowers
6. _____	8. _____	10. _____
7. _____	9. _____	11. _____

STRATEGY: Comparing and Contrasting

Decide if the sentence tells only about tree, only about flower, or about both. Circle the answer.

12. It is a living thing. tree flower both

Practicing Vocabulary

Write the word from the box that belongs in each group.

talking	plants	green	living

13. flowers, trees, _____

14. speaking, telling, _____

15. red, blue, _____

16. being, alive, _____

On another sheet of paper, draw a picture of yourself and a friend.
Write sentences that tell how you are alike and how you are different.

LESSON 18

Author's Purpose

An author is a person who writes a book.
An author has a reason for writing a story.
The author may want to make you laugh.
The author may want to tell you something.

Look at the book.
Draw a circle around the correct answer.

● Who is the author of this book?

Fred Green

Fred Baseball

Fred Games

ALL ABOUT GAMES
by Fred Green

■ What do you think this book is about?

food   games   animals

▲ Why do you think the author wrote
this book?

to be funny   to sell games   to tell about games

Tip **Read the name of the story or book. Look at the pictures. Then think about why the author wrote the book.**

Practicing Comprehension Skills

Read the sentences.
Think about why the author wrote "Hang Time."

Hang Time

by Kelly Brice

To play Hang Time, you need a ball.
Start counting when you toss it in the air.
Stop counting when you catch it.
Remember the number.
Let a friend toss the ball in the air.
See whose ball stays up the longest.

Draw a line under the answer.

1. Why did the author write Hang Time?

to tell about clocks   to tell about Hang Time

to make people sing songs

2. Why did the author write the words,
"Remember the number"?

to help you dance   to teach you numbers

so you will know whose ball was up the longest

3. Which book tells you about Hang Time?

Animal Stories   Ball Games   Dogs and Cats

Read this story.
Think about why the author wrote it.

The Great Catch

"Toss the ball to Pete!" Max called out.
"He'll drop it!" Kim said. "He always drops it!"
Pete felt bad. He wanted to be a good player.
He didn't want to let his team down.
Kim tossed the ball to Pete.
Pete watched the ball sail in the air.
He held up his glove. The ball fell in.
Pete waved the ball in the air and smiled.

Fill in the circle next to the answer.

4. Why does the author write that the ball fell into Pete's glove?

○ so we know that Pete dropped the ball

○ so we know the ball fell on the ground

○ so we know the ball landed in Pete's glove

5. Why does the author write that Pete smiled?

○ so we know that Kim is mad

○ so we know that Pete is happy

○ so we know that Max is sad

Draw a line under the best answer.

6. Why do you think the author wrote "The Great Catch"?

To make you cry.

To make you smile.

To tell you who to play with.

Practicing Vocabulary

Draw a line from the word to the group where it belongs.

stop

remember

sail

drop

7. think about again, recall

8. fall, let go

9. halt, quit

10. move, fly

Use another sheet of paper. Draw a picture of a game you like to play. Write some sentences that tell how to play the game.

Plot

Every story has a **plot**.
The plot is what happens in the story.
A plot has a beginning, a middle, and an end.

These pictures tell a story.

Beginning    Middle    End

Fill in the circle next to the correct answer.

● **What happened at the beginning?**

  ○ They went to the store. ○ They went on a picnic.

■ **What happened in the middle?**

  ○ It began to rain. ○ It began to snow.

▲ **What happened at the end?**

  ○ They went outside. ○ They ate in the car.

 When you read a story, try to figure out what happened at the beginning, middle, and end. Then you will know the plot.

Practicing Comprehension Skills

Read the story. Think about what happens in the beginning, middle, and end.

Going to a Pet Show

Rex is getting a bath.
"We're going to the pet show," Jack said.
"Rex will win the cleanest dog prize!"
said Dan.
Then Rex ran in the mud.
Jack and Dan took him to the pet show anyway.
Later Dan said, "I knew Rex would win a prize."
"Rex won the Dirty Dog prize!" Jack said.
The boys laughed. Rex barked.

1. Write 1, 2, or 3 next to each picture to show what happened at the beginning, middle, and end of the story.

2. What prize does Rex win?
   Fill in the circle next to the answer.

   ○ Clean Dog   ○ Fast Dog   ○ Dirty Dog

Read the story. Think about what happens at the beginning, middle, and end.

Space Dog

Boots was hungry.
He looked for food everywhere.
He even looked on a spaceship!
When Mom saw Boots, she smiled.
Then she gave Boots a big bone.
"You're going to be the first dog on the moon!" she said.

Fill in the circle next to the correct answer.

3. What happens at the beginning?

○   ○   ○

4. What happens in the middle?

○   ○   ○

5. What happens at the end of the story?
Fill in the circle next to the picture.

○    ○    ○

Practicing Vocabulary

Write a word from the box on each line.

_____

6. I think _____ nice.

_____

7. The _____ dog ate a bone.

_____

8. _____ going away today.

_____

9. The dog won a _____.

| hungry |
| we're |
| prize |
| you're |

On another sheet of paper, draw three pictures. Show the beginning, the middle, and the end of a trip you want to go on. Write a sentence to tell about each picture.

Character

Characters are the people authors write about in stories.
Authors tell what the characters do.
Authors tell how the characters feel, too.

Read the story. Think about the characters.

Megan likes to play with her toys.
She pretends they are her friends.
"Isn't this fun?" she asks them.
Then she laughs.

Fill in the circle next to the correct answer.

● Who is the character in this story?

○ a girl ○ a boy ○ a butterfly

■ What does the character like to do?

○ go to sleep ○ play with her toys ○ read maps

▲ How does the character feel?

○ sad ○ tired ○ happy

 Tip | **When you read, think about who the characters are. Think about what the characters do and how they feel.**

Practicing Comprehension Skills

Read the poem. Think about who the main character is.

Pete the Knight

by J. Patrick Lewis

"I want to be a knight," said Pete.
"I'll go to ask the King.
I want to be a knight because
I can do anything.
I ride a horse. I read big books.
I go to school. I sing!"

Fill in the circle next to the correct answer.

1. Who is the main character?

○ Megan   ○ Pete   ○ Jake

2. What does the character want to be?

○ a cowboy   ○ a teacher   ○ a knight

3. What will the character do to become a knight?

○ Ask the King.   ○ Run a race.   ○ Play a game.

Read the poem. Think about who the main character is.

Pete Meets the King

by J. Patrick Lewis

The King was brave. The King was kind.
He walked along the street.
"Good day. How do you do?"
he'd say to people he would meet.
He knew today he'd meet a knight.
The knight he met was Pete!

Draw a line under the correct answer.

4. Who is the most important character?

Pete   a horse   the King

5. What does the King do that shows he likes people?

The King asks people to visit his castle.

The King shows people his horse.

The King says, "Good day" to people.

6. How do you think the King feels as he walks down the street?

sleepy   silly   happy

7. Which words tell about the King?
Write the words on the line.

tired and hungry   brave and kind   loud and wild

_____

The king is _____ .

Practicing Vocabulary

Draw a line from the sentence to the word.

8. The _____ rode on his horse.   **anything**

9. He would do _____ the king asked.   **knight**

10. He was very _____.   **brave**

11. He _____ the king was his friend.   **knew**

Making the Reading and Writing Connection

On another sheet of paper, draw a picture of a story character you like. Then write two or three sentences about the character.

Setting

The **setting** is when and where a story happens. Pictures can help you tell where a story happens. So can words.

Look at the pictures. Draw a line under the words that tell you where or when the story happens.

● at the zoo

at the beach

■ at night

in the daytime

▲ Draw a circle around the picture that shows something that happened a long time ago.

Tip

When you read, think about when and where a story happens.

STRATEGY: Literary Elements: Setting   **85**

Practicing Comprehension Skills

Read the story. Think about where and when the story happens.

A Fish Story

Molly and her dad went fishing.
"This river is full of fish," Dad said.
"Look! I saw one splash in the water," Molly said.
"We'll catch our dinner," Dad told her.
Molly and her dad fished all day.
That night they ate fish for dinner.

Fill in the circle next to the answer.

1. Where does this story happen?

○ in school   ○ on a river   ○ in a city

2. When does this story happen?

○ in the winter   ○ a long time ago   ○ in the summer

3. What clue helped you tell when the story happens? Underline the answer.

Molly and Dad are wearing bathing suits.

Molly and Dad are wearing coats.

Molly and Dad are very cold.

Read the story. Think about when and where the story happens.

A Trip to the Zoo

It was windy outside.
"I'll wear my jacket," Lily said.
Lily and her mom rode on a bus.
They saw seals.
They saw big cats, too.
A cloud covered the sun.
Lily was glad she had her jacket.

Draw a circle around the correct answer.

4. Where does this story happen?

    at home   at the zoo   at school

5. When does this story happen?

    in the rain   on a hot day   on a chilly day

Fill in the circle next to the correct answer.

6. How can you tell where the story happens?

    ○ A cloud covered the sun.

    ○ Lily and her mom see different animals.

    ○ It is windy outside.

7. What in the story helps you tell when the story happens? Fill in the circle.

○ Lily and her mom ride a bus.

○ Lily and her mom go to the zoo.

○ Lily is glad she wore her jacket.

Practicing Vocabulary

Find a word in the box that matches each clue. Write it on the line.

I'll	windy	we'll	dinner

_____ **8.** we will

_____ **9.** I will

_____ **10.** breezy

_____ **11.** meal

Use another sheet of paper. Write a story about something two friends do together. Be sure to tell when your story happens. Tell where it happens, too.

22 Alphabetizing

The letters in the alphabet are in ABC order.
ABC order can make things easy to find.

Point to each letter. Say its name.
Think about the order of the letters.

a b c d e f g   h i j k l m n o p   q r s t u v   w x y z

Write the missing letters on the lines.

● e _____ g   j _____ l   p _____ r

■ c _____ e _____   r _____ t _____ v

▲ u _____ _____ x _____

Tip Say the abc's to yourself. Think about the
order of the letters. Then you will know
how to put things in ABC order.

Practicing Comprehension Skills

Read the story. Think about how the children will use ABC order.

A Color March

Meg put on a green hat.
"This is my size!" she said.
Alex put on an orange coat.
Holly put on a yellow dress.
"Now we can march," said Holly.
"We'll march with colors in ABC order!"

How will the children use ABC order?
They will put the color words in ABC order.

Circle the words that are in ABC order.

1. yellow   green   orange

   green   yellow   orange

   green   orange   yellow

2. Alex   Holly   Meg

   Holly   Alex   Meg

   Meg   Holly   Alex

Read the story. Find out how these children use ABC order.

An ABC Rainbow

We paint with our favorite colors.
Ann paints with red.
Mike paints with blue.
Jim paints with yellow.
We put the pictures in a line.
Look at our ABC rainbow!

Draw a line under the first letter of each color name. Then write 1, 2, and 3 to put each group of color words in ABC order.

3.

_____ yellow   _____ blue   _____ red

4.

green   pink   black   orange

Put the words in ABC order to write a sentence.

painting   love   rainbows   children   All

5. _____

Practicing Vocabulary

Draw a line from the word to the clue it matches.

march   6. things in a row

size   7. many colors

rainbow   8. parade

line   9. big or small

Get four sheets of paper. Use a different color to draw a picture on each sheet. Write the color name. Then put the colors in ABC order.

Picture Maps

A **picture map** shows you what a place looks like. It can also show you how to go from place to place.

This picture map shows a park.

● Circle what is at the front of the park.

■ Circle where you can feed the ducks.

Tip

Each picture on a picture map shows a place. Read a picture map by looking at each picture. Labels on the map may also help you.

Practicing Study Skills

Read the story.
Look at the picture map.

A Place to Play

This is where I like to play.
I climb up and up. Then I slide down.
I build a sand castle.
I swing so high I can touch the sky.
Mom waves from the bench.

Draw a line under the correct answer.

1. What does the picture map show?

farm   playground   town

Read each sentence.
Then show the place on the map.

2. Draw a ◯ circle around where you can swing.

3. Draw a △ triangle around where you can slide.

4. Draw a ☐ box around where you can play in the sand.

Read the poem. Look at the picture map.

Camp Fun

The Green family goes to Camp Fun.
At Camp Fun they ride, fish, and run.
First they work. Then they play.
They put up their tent in one day!
Soon they are tired. They want to eat.
Can you guess where they will meet?

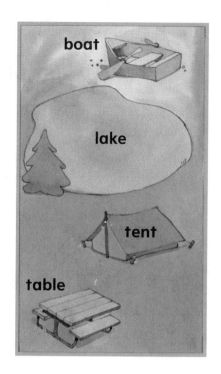

Draw a circle around the correct answer.

5. Where will the Green family sleep?

tent   boat   tree

6. Where will the Greens fish?

tree   table   lake

7. Where will the Green family meet to eat?

boat   table   tent

8. Fill in the circle next to the things you can do at Camp Fun.

○ eat   ○ fish   ○ shop

Write your answer on the line.

9. What would you like to do at Camp Fun?

_____

- -

_____

Practicing Vocabulary

Draw a line from the word to the group where it belongs.

slide

tired

bench

tent

10. sleepy, resting

11. hut, shed

12. swing, ride

13. chair, sofa

Use another piece of paper. Draw a picture map of a place where you have fun. First, draw pictures on your map. Then write a word that tells about each picture.

Picture and Bar Graphs

A **picture graph** or **bar graph** is a picture that tells a number story. Picture or bar graphs make it easy to count and compare things.

Mr. Lopez ordered four trumpets, two tubas, and three trombones for the school band.

This bar graph shows what Mr. Lopez ordered.

Horns for the Band

	1	2	3	4	5	6
Trumpets	🎺	🎺	🎺	🎺		
Tubas						
Trombones						

Use the bar graph to answer each question. Circle the correct answer.

● How many trumpets were ordered? **1   2   3   4**

■ How many tubas?   **1   2   3   4**

▲ How many trombones?   **1   2   3   4**

Tip | **Read the words and numbers on the bar graph. Find what you want to count. Then tell how many.**

Practicing Study Skills

Read the poem. Then look at the bar graph.

Flags in the Parade

The parade goes down the street.
Green and blue flags fly.
The flags go up.
The flags go down.
The marching feet go by.
Yellow flags and red flags, too.
I can see them. So can you!

Flags in the Parade

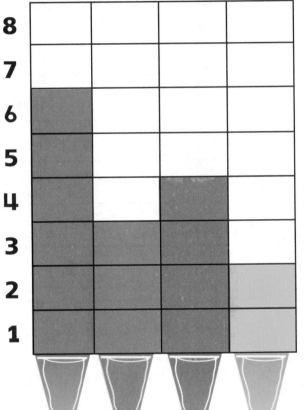

Read each sentence.
Circle **Yes** or **No**.

1. The parade has six red flags.

   Yes   No

2. The parade has three blue flags.

   Yes   No

3. There are more red flags than green flags.

   Yes   No

4. There are more yellow flags than green flags.

   Yes   No

Read the story. Look at the bar graph.

How Many Songs?

My class has a spring show.
We sing songs for our families.
The girls sing two songs.
The boys sing three songs.
Brad sings two songs by himself.
We sing some songs together.

How Many Songs?

	1	2	3	4	5	6
the girls	▨	▨				
the boys	▨	▨	▨			
Brad	▨	▨				
together	▨	▨	▨			

Write the number on the line.

_____

5. Everyone sings _____ songs together.

6. Brad sings _____ songs by himself.

Look at the bar graph again.
Write the number on the line.

7. At the spring show, the children sing

_____

- - - - - - - - -

_____ songs.

Practicing Vocabulary

Write the word from the box that matches each clue.

_____

- - - - - - - - -

_____   **8.** singing and dancing on stage

_____

- - - - - - - - -

_____   **9.** moms, dads, sisters, brothers

_____

- - - - - - - - -

_____   **10.** move

_____

- - - - - - - - -

_____   **11.** people marching down the street

| go |
| parade |
| show |
| families |

Making the
Reading
and
Writing
Connection

On another piece of paper, make a bar graph. Show what you and your friends might play in a band.

Level A Glossary

A **again** (ə gen´) once more; a second time

another (ə nuth´ər) one more

anything (en´ē thiŋ) any thing; something, no matter what

B **balloon** (bə loon´) a brightly colored rubber bag that is blown up with air

bears (berz) large animals with shaggy fur and short tails

bench (bench) a long, hard seat for a few people

bigger (big´ər) of greater size; larger

bird (burd) an animal that is covered with feathers and has two feet and two wings

blimp (blimp) an airship shaped somewhat like an egg

brave (brāv) not afraid of facing danger, pain, or trouble

bring (briŋ) to carry somewhere

C **cake** (kāk) a baked food that is made from a sweet batter

captain (kap´tən) the person in charge of a ship

catch (kach) to get by a hook, trap, or other tool

cook (kook) to prepare food for eating by using heat

cubs (kubz) baby lions, bears, whales, or other animals

D **different** (dif´ər ənt or dif´rənt) not the same

dinner (din´ər) the main meal of the day

dream (drēm) thoughts, pictures, or feelings that you have while you sleep

drop (dräp) to fall or let fall

F **families** (fam´ə lēz) groups made up of one or two parents and all their children

first (furst) before anyone or anything else

fish (fish) animals with fins and gills that live in water

flies (flīz) moves through the air by using wings

flowers (flou´ərz) the parts of a plant that have colored petals

fly (flī) to move through the air by using wings

found (found) discovered

G **go** (gō) to move along or pass from one place to another

green (grēn) having the color of growing grass

grow (grō) to make something get bigger

H **help** (help) to do something that is needed; to make things easier for someone

hive (hīv) a box where bees live

huge (hyōōj) very large

hungry (huŋ´grē) wanting or needing food

I **I'll** (īl) I will

K **kitchen** (kich´ən) a room for cooking food

kitten (kit´n) a young cat

knew (nōō or nyōō) was sure

knight (nīt) a man in the Middle Ages who was honored by the king

L **letters** (let´ərz) written messages, usually sent by mail

line (līn) a row of persons or things

living (liv´iŋ) having life; alive; not dead

lose (lōōz) to not have something anymore

M **made** (mād) created or put together

march (märch) to walk with regular, steady steps as soldiers do

mouth (mouth) the opening in someone's head through which food is taken in and sounds are made

N **nuts** (nuts) dry fruits with hard shells

P **parade** (pə rād´) people marching in a group

pick (pik) to choose or select

pilot (pī´lət) a person who flies an airplane

plane (plān) an aircraft that is kept up by the air on its wings

plants (plants) living things that cannot move around by themselves

plates (plāts) dishes used for food

pond (pänd) a small lake

prize (prīz) something that is given to the winner of a contest or game

Q **quit** (kwit) to stop doing something

R **rainbow** (rān´bō) a curved band of many colors across the sky

raincoats (rān´kōts) coats that protect people from the rain

reads (rēdz) understands the meaning of something written

remember (rē mem´bər) to be careful not to forget; to think of again

ring (riŋ) a thin band worn on the finger

rockets (räk´əts) long, narrow machines that fly or help things fly

S **sail** (sāl) to move in a smooth and easy way

sand (sand) the tiny grains that make up the ground of a beach or a desert

school (skōōl) a place for teaching and learning

seashore (sē´shôr) land by the sea

seed (sēd) the part of a plant that can grow into a new plant

shade (shād) to protect from light and heat

shoes (sho͞oz) coverings for the feet

show (shō) a performance of a play or music

size (sīz) how large or small a thing is

sky (skī) the upper part of the air around Earth

sled (sled) a low platform on runners that is used for riding over snow

sleep (slēp) to be at rest with the eyes closed

slide (slīd) to slip

smell (smel) to notice an odor through the nose; an odor that is noticed by the nose

snow (snō) soft, white flakes that form from tiny drops of water that freeze in the upper air and fall to earth

spider (spī´dər) a small animal with eight legs and a body made up of two parts

star (stär) an object in space that shines by its own light and is seen as a point of light in the night sky

stay (stā) to keep on being in the same place

stop (stäp) to keep from going on

swim (swim) to move through the water by moving the arms and legs

T **talking** (tôk´iŋ) saying words; speaking

teeth (tēth) white, bony parts that grow in the mouth and are used to bite and chew

tent (tent) a shelter made of material that is stretched over poles and attached to the ground

tired (tīrd) needing sleep or rest

U **use** (yo͞oz) to put into action

W **warm** (wôrm) keeping the body heat in

water (wôt´ər) a liquid that has no color and falls as rain to fill the oceans, rivers, and lakes

we'll (wēl) we will

we're (wir) we are

whale (hwāl or wāl) a very large animal that lives in the sea and looks something like a fish

why (hwī or wī) for what reason?

windy (win´dē) with a lot of wind

worm (wʉrm) a small, creeping animal that has a soft, slender body and no legs

Y **you're** (yo͝or or yo͞or) you are